Let's Celebrate

Memorial Day

MAY

by Clara Cella

Consulting Editor: Gail Saunders-Smith, PhD

CAPSTONE PRESS
a capstone imprint

Pebble Plus is published by Capstone Press,
1710 Roe Crest Drive, North Mankato, Minnesota 56003.
www.capstonepub.com

Library of Congress Cataloging-in-Publication Data
Cella, Clara.
   Memorial Day / by Clara Cella.
      p. cm. — (Pebble plus. Let's celebrate)
   Includes index.
   Summary: "Full-color photographs and simple text provide a brief introduction to Memorial Day"--Provided
by publisher.
   ISBN 978-1-4296-8732-4 (library binding)
   ISBN 978-1-4296-9390-5 (paperback)
   ISBN 978-1-62065-308-1 (ebook PDF)
   1. Memorial Day—Juvenile literature. I. Title.

   E642.C44 2013
   394.262—dc23   2012003825

Editorial Credits

Jill Kalz, editor; Kyle Grenz, designer; Marcie Spence, media researcher; Kathy McColley, production specialist

Photo Credits

Capstone Studio: Karon Dubke, 17, 19, 22; Dreamstime: Cheryl Casey, 21, John Alphonse, 13, Petr Svec, 7;
   iStockphoto: nicolesy, 15; North Wind Picture Archives, 11; Shutterstock: Frontpage, 1, Jim Barber, cover (flag),
   MBWTE Photos, cover (child), Tom Oliveira, 9, Vsevolod33, 5

Note to Parents and Teachers

The Let's Celebrate series supports curriculum standards for social studies related to culture.
This book describes and illustrates the Memorial Day holiday. The images support early readers
in understanding the text. The repetition of words and phrases helps early readers learn new
words. This book also introduces early readers to subject-specific vocabulary words, which are
defined in the Glossary section. Early readers may need assistance to read some words and to
use the Table of Contents, Glossary, Read More, Internet Sites, and Index sections of the book.

Printed in the United States of America in North Mankato, Minnesota.
042012   006682CGF12

Table of Contents

Hello, Memorial Day!

Memorial Day is a time

for remembering. It honors

U.S. soldiers who fought

and died for

our country's freedom.

5

Memorial Day is
on the last Monday of May.
It is a national holiday.
Government offices and
schools are closed that day.

On Memorial Day, U.S. flags
fly at half-staff. Lowering them
shows respect. People also
put flowers and flags
on soldiers' graves.

How It Began

Americans first celebrated

Memorial Day in the 1800s.

They called it Decoration Day.

It honored soldiers who had died

in the Civil War (1861–1865).

The name changed
to Memorial Day in 1882.
The holiday soon became
a day to honor U.S. soldiers
from all wars.

Memorial Day is a sad day.
But it's also a happy day.
Americans celebrate freedom
and give thanks for living
in a free country.

Let's Celebrate!

It's Memorial Day!

How will you celebrate?

Spend time with your family

and friends. Have a picnic.

Play sports or go to the beach.

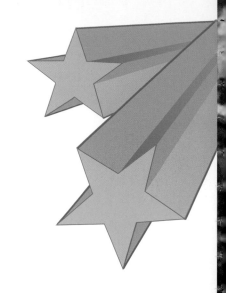

Honor soldiers by flying
a U.S. flag. Write letters
to soldiers serving today.
Thank them by sharing
a picture you drew.

Many cities have parades
on Memorial Day.
Listen to marching bands.
Remember the soldiers
who fought to keep us free.

Activity: Thank-You Wreath

Honor soldiers who have died by making a colorful thank-you wreath.

What You Need:

red, white, and blue construction paper

a pencil

scissors

a paper plate

a black marker

a glue stick

What You Do:

1. Use the pencil to trace your hands on the paper. Make at least eight hands.

2. Carefully cut them out.

3. Cut out the center of the plate.

4. Use the marker to write special words on the hands. Examples include "peace," "freedom," "brave," and "strong."

5. Glue the hands around the plate.

Read More

Dayton, Connor. *Memorial Day*. American Holidays.
New York: PowerKids Press, 2012.

Hamilton, Lynn. *Memorial Day*. American Celebrations.
New York: AV2 by Weigl, 2011.

Rissman, Rebecca. *Memorial Day*. Holidays and Festivals.
Chicago: Heinemann Library, 2011.

Internet Sites

FactHound offers a safe, fun way to find
Internet sites related to this book. All of the sites
on FactHound have been researched by our staff.

Here's all you do:

Visit *www.facthound.com*

Type in this code: 9781429687324

Super-cool stuff! Check out projects, games and lots more at
www.capstonekids.com

Glossary

celebrate—to honor someone or something on a special day

Civil War—(1861–1865) the battle between states in the North and South that led to the end of slavery in the United States

freedom—the right to do and say what you like

half-staff—halfway up a flagpole

soldier—a person who is in the military

Index

Word Count: 196
Grade: 1
Early-Intervention Level: 19